BULBS, CORMS, AND SUCH

MILLICENT E. SELSAM
PHOTOGRAPHS BY
JEROME WEXLER

William Morrow and Company
New York 1974

The author and photographer thank
Dr. Howard S. Irwin,
President of the New York Botanical Gardens,
for checking the text and photographs of this book.

Acknowledgment for Photographs
Malak Photographs Limited, 15, 17

Library of Congress Cataloging in Publication Data

Selsam, Millicent Ellis
  Bulbs, corms, and such.

  SUMMARY: A beginning botany book on the bulb family
of plants describing their structure and growth into such flowers
as daffodils, dahlias, and gladiolus.
  1. Bulbs (Botany)—Juvenile literature. 2. Bulbs—
Juvenile literature. 3. Corms—Juvenile literature.
4. Tubers—Juvenile literature. [1. Bulbs (Botany)]
I. Wexler, Jerome, illus. II. Title.
QK646.S48   584′.2   74-5939
ISBN 0-688-21822-9
ISBN 0-688-31822-3 (lib. bdg.)

To Ethel Heins,
for suggesting the idea for this book.

CONTENTS

BULBS

You probably have planted seeds
and watched new plants grow from them.
But have you ever planted a bulb?
A bulb can grow into a plant too.

5

FLESHY LEAVES

STEM

The onions in your kitchen are bulbs.
Each bulb is made up of a shortened stem,
which bears thick, fleshy leaves. Lots of food
is stored in these fleshy leaves and is used
by the plant that grows out of the bulb.

Often a flower bud is
in the center of a bulb.
The tulip, daffodil, and
hyacinth bulbs you buy
have flower buds
packed away inside.
This picture shows
a daffodil bulb
from the outside.

Now let's look inside.
A shortened stem is
at the bottom with
fleshy leaves attached to it
just as in the onion.
There is a flower bud
in the center.
It is a bit hard to see
in this picture.

FLESHY LEAVES

STEM

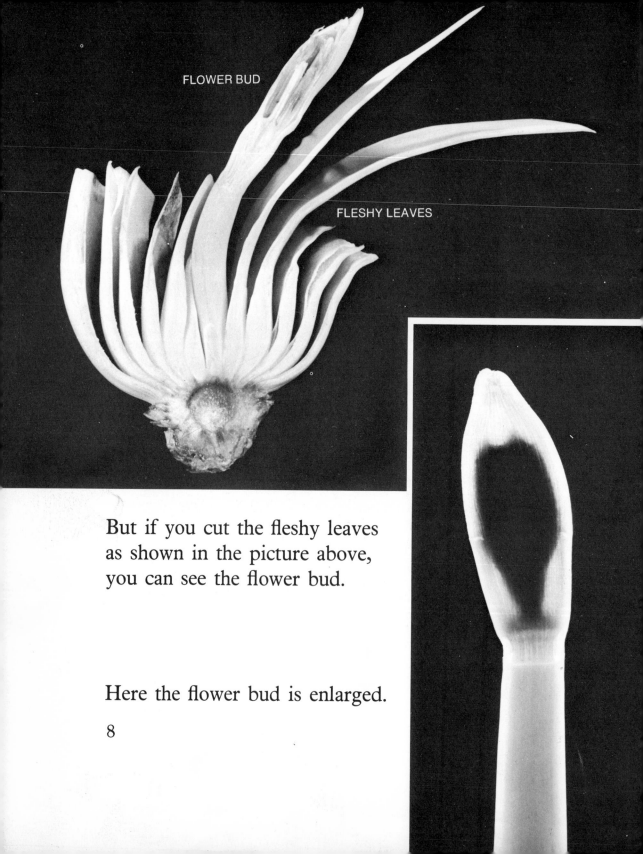

FLOWER BUD

FLESHY LEAVES

But if you cut the fleshy leaves as shown in the picture above, you can see the flower bud.

Here the flower bud is enlarged.

8

In the picture on the left you see
daffodil roots growing in a special glass
made for holding bulbs. Growing daffodils
indoors is possible, if you can keep them
in a cold place (about forty to fifty degrees)
while they are forming roots. When you plant
the bulb indoors, leaves and flower buds
come out of the bulb in six to eight weeks.
Outdoors they appear in the spring.

ROOTS

FLOWER BUD

LEAF

The buds open
into daffodil flowers
like this one.

SEED

Many kinds of daffodil flowers
set seeds. But if you plant
such seeds, you cannot be sure
that they will produce
the very same kind of daffodil.
The easier, faster, and
better way is to grow
the new plants from bulbs.

At the end of the season,
the original daffodil bulb
often forms several new bulbs.
In time, they separate
from the old bulb and grow
into individual plants.
Daffodils, therefore, multiply
from one season to the next.

11

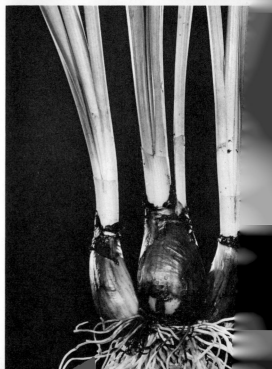

Here is a hyacinth bulb
cut so as to show
the flower buds inside.
The leaves in the center
enclose the buds.

When you remove
the leaves, you see
the flower buds clearly.
They have already
started to grow.

12

You can
grow
hyacinths
indoors
in a glass
just as
you do
daffodils.

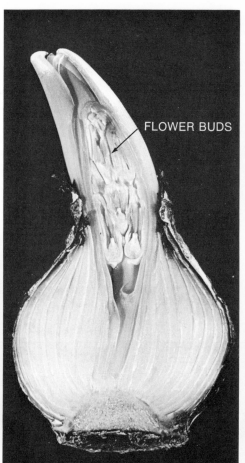

FLOWER BUDS

Flowers and leaves
come out of the bulb.
This growth uses up
the stored food
in the bulb.

After flowering,
the bulb
shrinks in size.
Notice how
this bulb has
grown smaller
and fallen
into the water.
Before it was
held up by
the neck
of the glass.

At the end
of the season,
this hyacinth bulb
has produced
two side bulbs.

Hyacinths bloom in the spring.

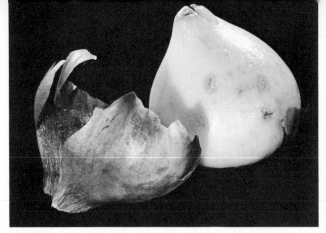

Here is a tulip bulb. The papery
outside leaves have fallen off.

This cut through the bulb shows
how thick the fleshy leaves are.
You can find the flower bud
in the center, if you look carefully.

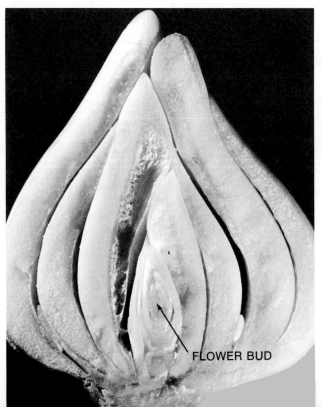

FLOWER BUD

Leaves and
flower buds
emerge and

grow into tulip plants like the ones pictured here.

17

The old tulip bulb dies and falls apart,
but several new bulbs are left in its place.

18

All the spring flowering bulbs, such as daffodils, hyacinths, and tulips, go through the same cycle of growth. The bulbs are planted in the fall. The roots grow rapidly and keep growing until the ground freezes. The bulbs, with roots already formed, stay in the ground all winter.

In the spring there is a second period of growth, when leaves and flowers come out of the bulb. Then comes an important time in the life of the bulb. The flowers may die, but the leaves continue to live. They manufacture food from carbon dioxide in the air and water from the soil with the aid of energy from sunlight. This food travels down to the bulb and is stored there in the fleshy leaves. At *this* time the new flower bud forms in the bulb. For this reason, the plants must be watered after flowering to keep the leaves from dying.

Finally the tops die down. Nothing is left above the soil. But underground there is a fat bulb or several new bulbs ready to spring to life again. Inside each bulb there is a flower bud and food packed around it in the fleshy leaves.

19

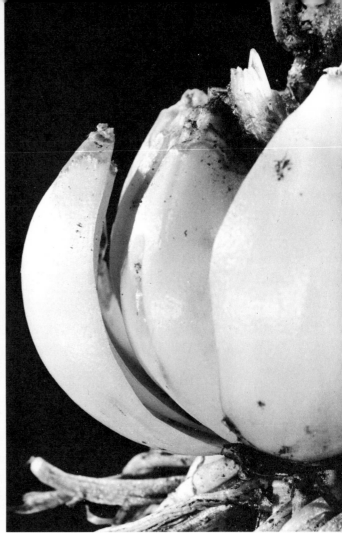

Lily bulbs stay in the ground all winter too.
They are hardy like daffodils, hyacinths, and tulips.
But lilies bloom in the summertime instead
of in the spring. The bulb looks like a cluster
of fleshy leaves. The close-up on the right
shows how thick they can be.

Lily bulbs do not have
preformed flowers in
the bulb as is the case
with hyacinths,
daffodils, and tulips.
Stems and leaves
come out of the bulb.

Flower buds appear later.

21

The buds open into lily flowers.

If you dig up this lily plant
in the late summer,
you can find tiny little bulbs
on the part of the stem
that is underground.

SOIL LEVEL

TINY NEW BULB

ORIGINAL BULB

Pull off one of these bulbs
and plant it. It soon produces
a root and will grow into
a full-sized lily bulb in
about three to four years.

23

TINY BULB

ROOT

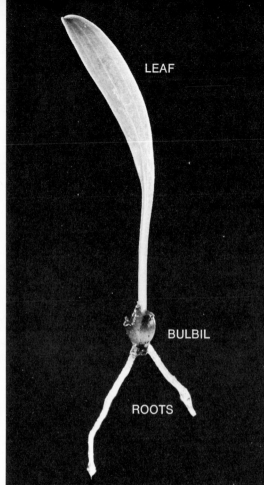

Some lilies also form little bulbs, called "bulbils,"
where the leaves join the stem. When they are ripe,
they can be broken off easily and planted.
If not picked off, they fall to the ground.

When a bulbil falls to the soil or is planted,
it sends out roots and starts to grow
into a full-sized bulb that will flower.

24

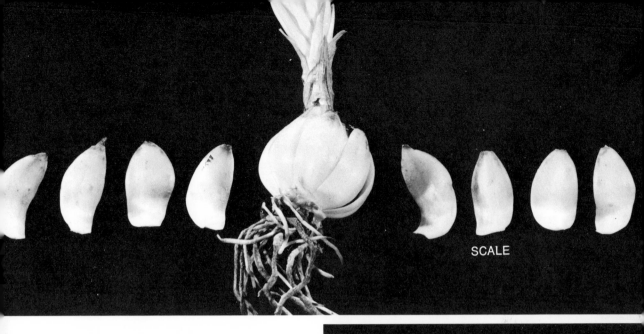

SCALE

Even the scales of the
lily bulb can grow into
new plants. You can
remove as many as half
the scales and plant them
in moist sand or sand
mixed with peat moss.

Tiny little bulbs form
on the old scales.
They grow into new
lily plants that will form
bigger and bigger bulbs
until flowering size
is reached.

25

LEAF

NEW BULB

SCALE

ROOT

CORMS

This gladiolus bulb may look like other bulbs
on the outside, but inside it is different.
Instead of fleshy leaves, there is a solid mass
of stem tissue. It is called a "corm."
Like a bulb, it is full of stored food.

Here you can see the stem tissue in the center and the food packed around it in the light areas.

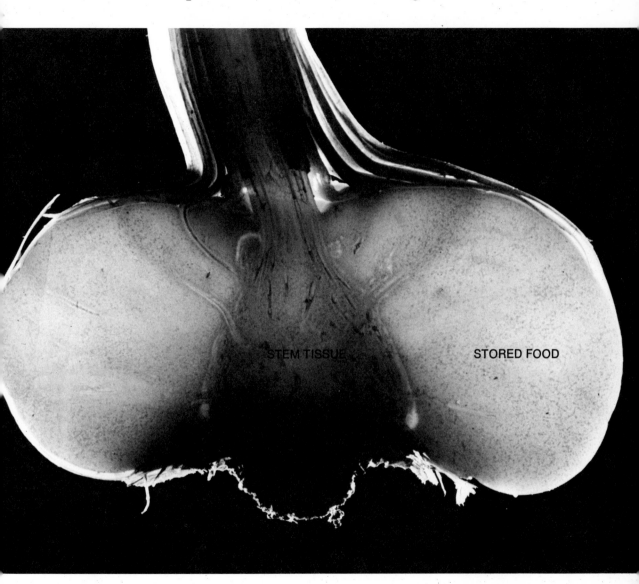

Notice the buds at the top.
Roots grow from the bottom.

Sword-shaped
leaves come
from the buds.

The gladiolus gets
its name from the
Latin word *gladius,*
which means *sword.*

Gladiolus flowers
bloom on long spikes.

The food in the corm is used up as the plant grows. It shrivels. But on top of it a new corm forms. At the end of the summer, this new corm has to be lifted from the ground, stored where it will not freeze, and then planted outside again the following spring. It is called "tender" for this reason.

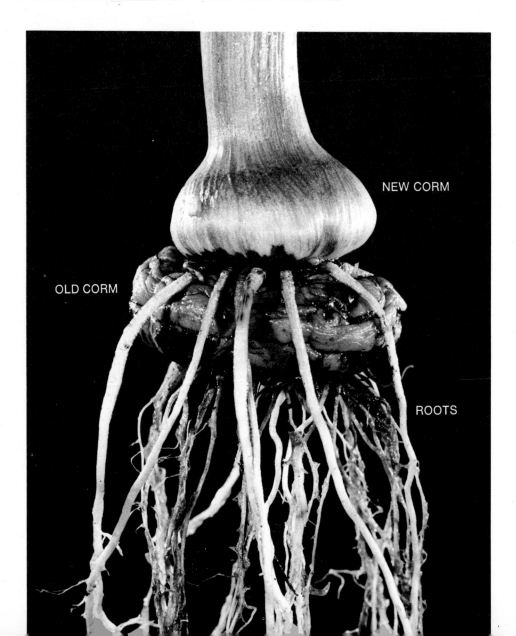

NEW CORM

OLD CORM

ROOTS

TINY
NEW CORMS

Tiny little corms form all around the base
of the new corm. They can be pulled off and
kept for planting time the following year.
In two to four years they become full-sized corms.

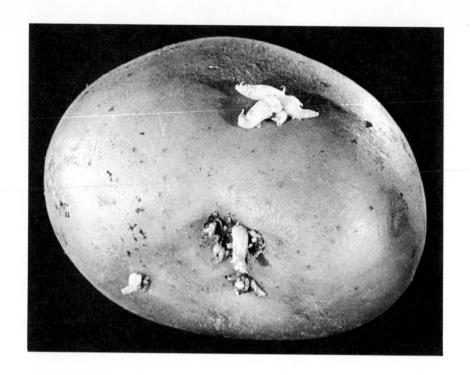

TUBERS

The tuber is another kind of underground
swollen stem that can grow into a new plant
or plants. The potato in your kitchen is a tuber.
It has eyes, or places on the tuber where
there are buds. Each bud can grow into
a new potato plant. The rest of the potato
is full of stored food, which the plant
uses as it grows. This stored food is also
a good source of food for you.

The tuberous begonia
gets its name from
the fact that it forms
tubers underground.
These tubers are round.
The buds are in
the hollow of the tuber.

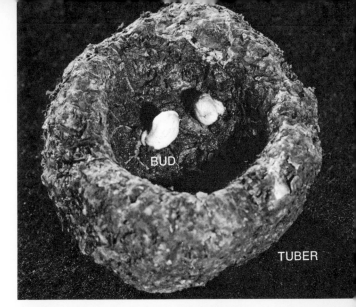

BUD

TUBER

This tuber has been
cut across the middle.
You can see how plump
the stored food makes it.
As the top grows,
the food in the tuber
is used up.

33

PIECE WITH BUD

CUTTING

ROOTS

But then the leaves manufacture more food, which
passes down through the stem and back to the tuber.
The tuber gets larger every year and does not
split up or form more little tubers on the side.
To get more plants, the original tuber may be cut
into pieces. As long as there is a bud on the piece,
it can grow into a new plant.

New plants also grow from seed or from pieces of
the stem (cuttings), which root when they are planted.

34

Begonia flowers blossom in gorgeous colors.

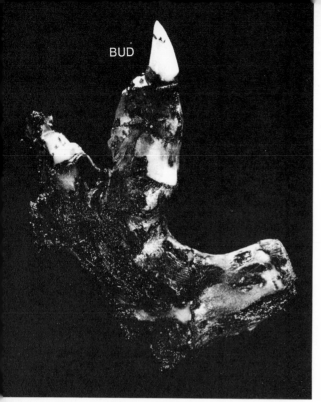

BUD

RHIZOMES

The rhizome is another kind
of underground stem
with food packed in it.
It also has buds from
which new plants can grow.
It is different from
a tuber, because it grows
horizontally underground.

Here is the rhizome
of the canna plant.

ROOTS

Roots grow down
into the soil.

Leaves
grow up.

FLOWER STALK

The flower
stalk develops.

37

Canna flowers
are large and
many colored.

This picture shows
the root system
of the canna plant
at the end of
the summer.

Here the roots
are removed, and
you can see new buds
that have formed
at the sides of
the old rhizome.
The following year
new canna plants will
grow from these buds.

39

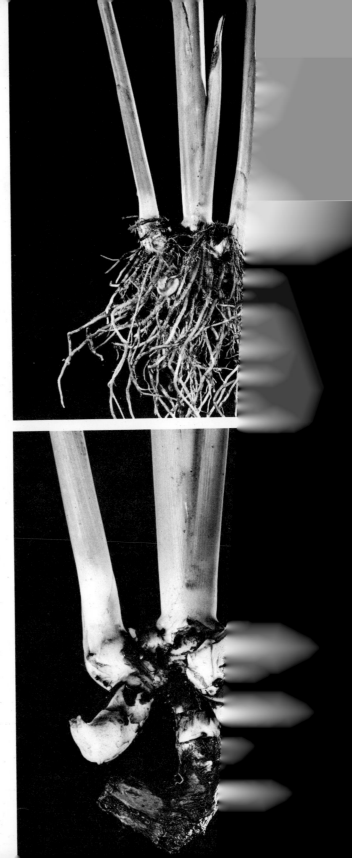

TUBEROUS ROOTS

Some underground
roots store a lot
of food too.

They are called
tuberous roots.
The sweet potato
that you eat
is an example.

There are buds
all over the
sweet potato
as there are on
the plain potato.
These buds
can grow into
new plants by
using the food
stored in the
fleshy roots.

On many tuberous roots, there are no buds
on the root itself. Instead, buds form on the base
of the old stem at the top of the tuber.

The dahlia tuber has
buds only at the top.

The buds grow into
stems and leaves.

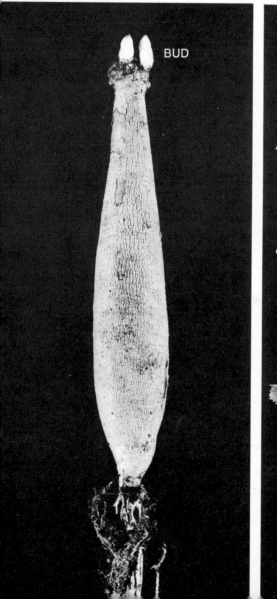

Then dahlia flowers bloom.

NEW TUBER

OLD TUBER

Meanwhile, underground, the old tuber gradually disappears, because the food in it is used up. But new tubers form. All summer long the leaves of the dahlia manufacture food, which travels down to the roots and is stored there.

If you plant a single dahlia tuber in the spring, you will find a whole clump of roots when you dig it up in the fall. These roots can be divided into separate tubers and planted in the spring.

NEW CLUMP

Every one of the plants in this book has
a way of producing new plants without seeds.
All of them have beautiful flowers and
are not hard to grow once you learn how.
Simple directions are given on the following pages.

DIRECTIONS FOR GROWING

Begonia, tuberous

Start the tubers indoors in March or April. The buds are in the hollow of the tuber, so plant the tubers concave side up. Press them into plastic trays filled with peat moss. Keep the trays evenly moist, and place them in a warm, light place. When there are two leaves showing, transfer each tuber to a pot containing $\frac{1}{3}$ peat moss, $\frac{1}{3}$ potting soil, and $\frac{1}{3}$ vermiculite (these three ingredients can be bought in the five-and-ten-cent store). When warm weather comes, set the pots outside in a shady place. In the fall, dig up the whole plant. Allow it to dry thoroughly. Then break off the stems. Place the tubers in boxes or bags containing dry peat moss, and keep them in a cold but not freezing place till the next spring.

Canna

The rhizomes cannot stand freezing weather. Plant the tuberous roots indoors in flat trays, and keep in a warm place till the rhizomes begin to sprout. Then, in May, plant them in the garden four inches deep. Cannas need rich soil in a sunny place and plenty of water. In the fall, dig up the rhizomes after the first frost. Allow them to dry. Then store them in boxes containing dry peat moss. Keep the boxes in a cool dry place.

Daffodil

Plant the bulbs early in the fall three times as deep as they are thick. Daffodil bulbs tend to multiply and spread, so that in a few years you can expect lots of daffodils even though you may start with only a few. Keep watering and fertilizing the daffodil plants after the flowers have disappeared, for the new flower bud forms at this time.

To grow daffodils indoors, buy varieties especially selected for growing in pots. Plant them in the fall in pots containing potting soil, which can be bought in the five-and-ten-cent store. Put the pots in a cold but not freezing place. Forty to fifty degrees is the best temperature. You can put them in an unheated cellar or in the back of the refrigerator (if there is room). Roots form during this cold period. After about six weeks, bring the pots into a well-lighted room.

Dahlia

Plant the tubers in the spring when the weather has warmed up. Lay the single tubers on their sides about six inches below the surface of the ground in a sunny place. Cover the tubers with three inches of soil, and as the shoots grow fill in with more soil. Fertilize and water them well. In the fall, dig up the clump. Allow the tubers to dry. Then store them in a box with dry peat moss between them. Put the box of tubers in a cold place as, for example, a cellar where the temperature will stay between forty and forty-five degrees. The tubers must not be allowed to freeze.

Gladiolus

In the spring, plant the corms so that they will be covered with four inches of soil in a sunny place in the garden. In the fall, lift the corms, cut off the tops, and allow them to dry in an airy place for a few weeks. Then remove the old corms from the plump new corm at the top. Also save the cormels (small corms produced by the large corm). Store large and small corms in paper bags at a temperature between forty and forty-five degrees. Save till spring. Plant the large corms in the garden, where you want the bloom to show. Plant the cormels in an out-of-the-way place, where they can grow bigger. They need about three years to get to blooming size, but remember to dig them up each fall and store them, so that they will not freeze.

Hyacinth
Plant the bulbs in the fall. Place deep enough in the ground so that they can be covered with five inches of soil. The bulbs may stay in the ground year after year, but the flowers get smaller. If you want only large-size hyacinth flowers, you must plant new bulbs every year. If you want to grow hyacinths indoors, follow the directions for daffodils.

Lily
Lily bulbs should be planted as soon as they are bought to prevent the fleshy roots from drying out. They can be planted in the fall or early spring. Place them deep enough to cover with five inches of soil. Spread some fertilizer on the ground above the bulbs, and water the soil well. The bulbs can stay in the ground all winter. They are hardy and do not freeze. They need a soil that drains the water off quickly. If your soil is a heavy clay that stays wet and sticky after a rainfall, add peat moss to lighten it.

Tulips

Plant the bulbs in the fall deep enough so that you can cover them with ten inches of soil. Tulips bulbs produce the biggest flowers the first spring after planting. Afterward the bulbs become smaller, which makes the flowers smaller. Deep planting (ten inches) prevents the tulip bulbs from multiplying too much and keeps the flowers larger for a longer time. But deep planting can be dangerous, if the soil is heavy and holds water for a long time. Such soil can be loosened by adding peat moss. This treatment will help the water to drain away so that it will not remain around the bulbs and rot them.

To grow tulip bulbs indoors, follow the directions for indoor daffodils.

Note: It is best to spend the money to buy top-quality bulbs because, as you have learned in this book, the flower bud is inside the bulb and was formed when the plant was growing the previous year. If it was grown with care, the flower bud will be of good size, and there will be plenty of stored food around it. You can also be sure that top-quality bulbs were handled well and kept in good storage conditions until ready for sale.